AF211512

# Discdogging

Tips and tricks for beginners and advanced learners

---------------------------------------------------------------

Author:
Julia Zimmermann

Illustrations:
H.-P. Losert, Nadine Schott

Translation help:
Sally Laws-Werthwein

Set and layout:
Fabian Dreyer

Print, production and publishing:
books on demand GmbH, D-22848 Norderstedt

Editor:
Verlag Dr. Scriptor OHG, D-67459 Böhl-Iggelheim

Sponsored by and thanks to:
dcast S.r.l., Diego Marchetti, Via del Giordano 9,
I-26100 Cremona, Italy

2010
ISBN 978-3-8391-9461-4

Julia Zimmerman is devoted to teaching people how to have a better relationship with their dogs.
She has comitted her life to becoming one of the best disc dog trainers in the world.
There are few who understand how to teach a dog like Julia.

Zak George
(Animal Planet host)

Julia is one of the premier disc dog trainers/competitors/performers in the world! She combines the largest repertoire of throws by any woman in the world, with some of the most innovative moves by anyone; to always deliver a unique and professional routine. Her dedication to the sport, the love and devotion to her canine companions, and her training experience truly makes her a joy to know, and to learn from.

Lawrence Frederick
2008 AWI Disc Dog World Champion

Fans of disc doggin', and future fans of our great sport are lucky to have this book available. Penned by one of the most respected and well known European teams, this book is a must have for ANY disc dogger. No matter if you are brand new to the sport, or have been involved for years, just thumbing through the pages often turns up something new, and Julia's unique perspective on the sport is reflected in her writing and obvious passion for her dogs. A MUST HAVE for anyone involved in disc doggin'!!

Matt DiAno
3 times UFO Disc Dog World Champion 2006-2008

This year I was fortunate enough to have Julia Zimmerman come stay a few days with her dogs at my house. What a great experience getting to play disc with her and her great dogs away from the tournament scene. She quickly taught me some great new tricks that I have already started to incorporate into my routines. Julia has some of the most innovative disc throwing skills in the sport and you better watch closely as you might miss one there are so many great ones.

Mark Muir
USDDN Disc Dog World Champion 2008
Rocket and Gipper and Irish
www.georgiairishdiscdogs.com

# List of contents:

Dear readers,

Discdogging – playing Frisbee with the dog for partner – is a modern and interesting to watch movement pattern and sport with barking four-legged friends , that can be operated from easygoing leisure-time activity without ambitions to participation at competitions.

It´s always fun and activity keeps in good shape – people and dogs.

Healthy and active dogs, who have the will to learn and own retrieving ability ( most dogs have it, it just need to be encouraged and stipulated ) are able to learn Discdogging. The basic rules and requirements are the same for every kind of playing Frisbee with a dog, independent from the planed level to go.

Our author Julia Zimmermann writes in memorable words and shows on numerous – and instructive pictures how it works. All expert and experienced, succeeded practitioner no Discdogging interested will get bored, on the contrary: the lecture whet the appetite of check it out and lures to the park, the beach wherever you can practice this wonderful game and improve it step by step.

To our readers and their dogs we wish optimal conditions for practice, success in built a team with each other and lots of fun with the flying disc, who really means a whole world of activity of it´s own.

Verlag Dr. Scriptor OHG (editor)

About the author:

Julia Zimmermann is living with their dogs Lara and Jetman in Karlsruhe / Germany. In 2001 Lara a Border Collie entered her life. During one of her long walks with Lara she got known Jochen Schleicher ( initiator of dogfrisbee sport in Germany ) and therewith dogfrisbee too.

Not even one and a half year later Lara and Julia participated at their first competition and they gained a good placement from the first moment on. Till today they show constantly great performance at competitions. They are one of the best European teams  and that has it´s reason. Who is allowed to see Lara and Julia live on field , sees a team. They not just play ” with each other ” but rather more “ for each other “ . They play dogfrisbee, they not execute it.

Devoid of pressure to succeed for the dog Julia is always anxious to train her dog safe and never to lose sight of health. She owns the rare gift to realize the natural talent of a dog, create a trick out of it and always refine herself.

In 2003 Jetman joined the pack. A Border Collie from a rescue center. He is not a easy to handle dog, who found, cause of Julia´s friendly manner, tons of patience and activity back to life.

With this book you get a wide knowledge around the dogfrisbee sport. If you enjoy dogfrisbee you get with this opus lots of suggestions to develop various tricks and throws. It salvages a great treasure of experience and will help you to realize what your trainings mate offers you and what you can make out of it.

I am glad I was allowed to got known Julia Zimmermann at the ButchCassidyCup 2001. To watch her is always an inspiration for my own conduct .

Conny Sawicki (off-Handteam)

# Preamble

## What is discdogging?

Discdogging is a special kind of canine-human sport or leisure activity for dogs and humans.
Discdogging comes from the USA and has existed there for more than 20 years.


How it all started:

It all started with flying plates. Around the turn of the century American students turned over a cake pan from the bakery "Ma Frisbee" and threw it to each other. In combination with the principle of an aeroplane wing at the end of the 50s it became the first Frisbee it became. Wham'OFrisbee bought the patent and protected the name Frisbee as trademark. Because progress does not even stop for Frisbee discs, the then student, Alex Stein, discovered his affection for so- called Fastbacks. These discs are different in weight and diameter to conventional discs, they are smaller and lighter and so it is possible to throw them faster and more accurately over short distances andthus they stay in the air for a longer time. As an enthusiastic Frisbee player Stein used every free moment to practise with friends at the park and he became really good! In summer 1971 a new companion stepped into his life. His name was Ashley Whippet, a male Whippet who looked like a greyhound (just smaller).This dog was just as good as hismaster and naturally also with the small missiles which look like UFOs. Ashley Whipped studied their trajectory every day at the park and one day he made an attempt to catch one. Alex and his friends observed how the dog started to spurt, came closer and closer to the Frisbee and at the right moment jumped to catch the Frisbee in the air. All of them applauded excitedly and a new sport was born.

Alex and Ashley practised every free minute with increasing enthusiasm and they got better every day. They developed more and more tricks out through different throwing techniques and so the crowds of spectators increased. After a lot of praise and a little mocking from friends and relatives, Alex considered how he could make the discdogging sport known in the whole country or even better worldwide. Therefore he decided to smuggle the dog and himself into a baseball stadium to show what they had learned. For this historical event he did not choosejust any location, he chose the "Dodger Stadium" in Los Angeles,where on 08/05/1974 the Dodgers and the Reds met for a national Championship in front of a lot press reporters. Dogs are not allowed inside the stadium , but that was no problem for Alex .He just took off Ashley,s leash and his dog followed him faithfully hidden by the crowd. Just before the beginning of the ninth innings was the right time. Alex and Ashley jumped over the fence round the field and started their show. They began with spectacular throws and the spectators started to applause uncontrollably. Both Ashley´s running speed of 60km/h and  his over 2 meter jumps excited the spectators more and more, and it was a delight to watch this spectacle. TV stations commented live and the radio stations described to the listeners what was happening on the field. After a few minutes the security forces stopped Alex Stein , but what Alex Stein achieved with this action was the beginning of a new era of dog sport. Appearances on TV followed, shows at the Super Bowl XII, radio interviews, as the first non-humanbeing a portrait of Ashley was printed in the "People Magazine", he got his own credit card, was the mascot for the football team L.A.Rams and he got a place at the "Dog Fancy" Hall of Fame for being dog frisbee world champion three times .

**Now you are probably just as wise as before!**

## So, now for an explanation:

In Discdogging we play Frisbee (or flying disc) with a dog and not with an other person.

And why should we do that?.... You will now ask your self.

All right, let´s take a look:

-because dogs love to hunt and here we have a great game to train their instinct
-because you can play nearly everywhere without any special preparation
-because it is very versatile... from just retrieving to playing a routine for championships, everything is possible. According to every liking!
-because your dog has to use his brain
-because you develop an intensive relationship with your four-footed partner - the more we develop it the more both partners have to pay attention and communicate with each other
-because it is practical for every dog who loves to play (if you want to enter competitions your dog should be in good health and you should give him a reasonable amount of training, of course)
-because most dogs love to catch things in the air
-because people have a lot of fun with this leisure-time activity
-because for us dog owners it is an advantage that we do not need another person as a partner to play the game with the flying disc, we have our dog
-because playing Frisbee is more than simply throwing to and from each other
-because it is a real sport for people too! To know how to throw properly is the essential part of for Discdogging! And that needs a lot of practise!!
-because we can play whenever we want to when we have time

O.K. If you now say: How dumb is that?... Then lay the book aside.
For the rest of you: Welcome to the world of Discdogging!!
Even if you are still sceptical.... completely unathletic people can tell you:

## IT´S ADDICTIVE!!
....not just for your dog... but for you too.

Before we start I would like to say something about my book: It DOES NOT contain perfect formulae!! What you will read here are possibilities or suggestions. You and your dog may find everything to be completely different. You are working with a living creature and these are all individuals as is well known.

# 1. Basic principles for the start

Even if you just want to use Discdogging for throwing something other than a ball to your dog:

**Use special dog discs!!!**

Your dog and his health will thank you for this!

## 1.1 A little explanation about discs

**Special dog discs? - YES!**

Imagine if you had to catch  hard plastic discs or a 200g heavy disc with your mouth!
-OUCH!
I would say: No thanks!

…well…personally I would not even want to catch the dog disc like this…but then.. I don´t even catch balls in my mouth!
Where is the difference then?

**"discs for people"**
Mostly they are made of hard plastic or are very big and heavy with a very deep rim. Hard plastic is hard, as the name suggests.  If it hits dog teeth these can break easily.
Also this material splinters when the dog bites it as he catches it. Furthermore, the edges are often sharp and can injure the tongue and flews. To think that my dog has a splinter somewhere in his mouth, throat or anywhere else would scare me.
Often the discs are very heavy. If the disc hits the teeth or the dog anywhere else,  it is quite dangerous.

## "dog discs"

There are several different designs available, depending on your personal preferences and depending on whether you enter competitions or are just interested in a leisure activity.
They all have one thing in common:

- they are not too big and heavy
- they are smooth and flexible
- they don´t have sharp edges
-they don´t break or splinter

Some of the models

### -Dogstar/Fastback

This disc is based on the American Fastback. The Dogstar and the Fastback disc have good flying characteristics.Thus they are very good for tricks, different throwing technics and long throws. With the right throwing technique they level off in the air allowing the dog to focus and catch them very well.

### - Dogstar Chrusher

This disc is based on the frostbite disc. Due to a higher percentage of rubber the disc is smoother. So it is suitable for dogs with a strong bite (it is not destroyed so quickly). Even dogs with a sensitive mouth love to play with this disc, which is resistant against the cold. Harder discs can crack in wintertime. The Crusher can be used at temperatures below freezing point.

### - K9 Flex-FastbackFrisbee

This is a stable, flexible disc specially for Discdogging. Depending on how hard the bite of the dogs is, it can be very expensive to play with this disc. A dog with a strong bite can destroyit in a short time.

### - Frostbite

A disc with a higher rubber percentage, which is resistant to freezing.

## - Dogobie

These are discs made completely out of rubber. They are gentle to the teeth and are for dogs which do not have too strong a bite and they are almost indestructible. Because of the material they are very floppy, so they do not fly particularly well. They fit into nearly every pocket and are definitely suitable for a short game (instead of a ball) every now and then.

## - Nylon discs

These are discs made out of nylon with a strengthened rim. They are light and flexible  and are suitable for dogs with a sensitive mouth for a short game on a walk and for puppies.
Right now there is an extensive variety of dog discs available.

The Dogstar, Fastback and Frostbite disc have good flying characteristics. Thus they are very good for tricks, diffenrent throwing technics and long throws. With the right throwing technique they level off in the air allowing the dog to focus and cath them very well.

The durability of a disc depends on the dog and his bite. But it is better to have broken discs than a dog with an injured mouth.

So the choice is not that easy.

**Here are some points to consider when making a choice:**
-You want the disc as a change from other toys?
-Your dog has a sensitive mouth?
-You don´t want to make the effort or don´t have the time to learn how to throw
-First of all you would like to see if your dog likes the new toy

Experience has shown that in this case Dogobie and Nylon discs are the right choice.
-You already like the game with the disc?
-You would like to throw longer distances?
-You have got the discdogging bug and you want to learn how to throw and do tricks with your dog? Perhaps even compete in championships?

For this purpose you can use the Dogstar and K9 discs. Finally the decision between the two is a question of finance and your personal preferences.

## 1.2 Everything depends on the throwing technique

With Frisbee playing it is the same as with every sport... you should learn it correctly (except if you are a natural talent).

Only if you have learned to throw correctly is the game not dangerous for the dog.

Ask the Ultimate Teams at Highschools or Universities for training.

## 1.3 Safety first- most important: safety !!

No matter how much you indulge in discdogging... the dog's safety is the most essential point, of course.

This means you should resist the temptation of playing on a nearby rough field with holes ...

...the danger of your dog suffering an injury by stepping into a hole or something similar is very high.
Also the ground should not be too hard or be coated with asphalt...
but this is fairly obvious

Warm your dog up before a game and let him run freely afterwards. In this way you can avoid ligament and muscle injuries.
Throw away damaged and chewed discs. This avoids injuries inside the mouth of your dog.

Don't demand too much of your dog. A dog which is completely involved in a game rarely stops if he is exhausted. Stop the game at the right time. It's better to play more often for short lengths of time.

Don't feed your dog directly before the game, otherwise there is the danger that your dog will get an upset stomach.

After each game check your dog for any possible injuries.

You have decided to compete in championships?

Take the following into consideration:

Your dog is an athlete! In two weeks from zero to a hundred – is perhaps possible -but think about the fact that we often practise many years in a sport until we are ready to take part in competitions. It´s the same with your dog and you also want to have enjoyment with your dog for many years.

With a sensible training build-up over an adequate period of time, you and your dog will enjoy this sport for a long time. And that is the most important thing!

The number of discdoggers providing information is increasing all the time. The addresses are given at the end.

## 1.4 Etiquette

It´s not easy to be a dog owner.

At this point I would like to touch upon some aspects, which should go without saying (at least from my point of view).

Everyone, who plays dog Frisbee, is a representative of the sport. Outsiders cannot differentiate between hobby and sport. Therefore you should show consideration for your surroundings including the people and dogs there.

You like to be treated the same way too, right?

Keep the environment clean: pick up what your dog leaves behind. No matter if someone has seen it or not.

Make sure your dog behaves correctly. Incorrect behaviour can be embarrassing or even become dangerous!

Alright, that was a lot of basic points, but there are always points to be observed and considered. All of this is important for keeping your dog in good health, can prevent needless frustration and increase the fun factor significantly.

And one more thing, before we continue:

Every dog has its own way of learning. So don´t give up, if it does not work the first time. Be creative. I´m sure you will find a way to achieve your goal. If you have worked hard for a long time on something, you can be much more proud, if you finally reach your goal.

**Enough of the theory . Let´s get to the practical part!**

# 2. Throwing techniques

**Yes I know…now you want get started with your four-legged friend!**

Sorry, but I must insist: no matter whether you play as a leisure activity or as a sport, no matter which disc you use, everything depends on the thrower. To clarify: the better you throw, the better the disc flies, the better the dog catches it and the safer it is for your dog. This way you and your dog will have so much more fun.
Now you will ask yourself: How should I learn this from a book?
Good question! It is really best to find someone who can train you. Nevertheless I have attempted to demonstrate the throwing techniques in writing and in pictures.

## 2.1 Backhand

Really everyone knows this as the "beach.throw ". Now you will say: "That´s very easy". But don´t forget:
The disc should fly so that your dog can catch it safely.

- **Position**
- Stand easy with your legs slightly apart.

- **Grip**

Put 4 fingers into the rim of the disc with the thumb on the upside. Don´t hold the disc too loosely and not to tightly. If you hold the disc to loosely it will waver through the air. If you hold the disc too tightly, it will not leave your hand when you release it.

Then you hold the disc with the upside slightly slanting away from your body.

Hold the disc like this at the moment of release too. In this way the disc will fly in a more stable manner in the air.

### -Technique

Bend over slightly. This way there is a distance between yourself and the disc, in case your dog should be too enthusiastic to get the disc, so that he does not snap at you . What is more, you can swing out more widely to give the disc more drive.

Guide the disc in front of you in the direction of your free arm. Now move the throwing arm with a smooth movement into the release position. The release position should be at shoulder height, the arm shows in the direction in which the disc should fly . Don´t forget to hold the disc in a slightly slanting position. Now throw the slanting disc with a spin (coming from the wrist). You can compare the spin with the technique used in table soccer .

A correct backhand is one of the most difficult throws .

## 2.2 Sidearm

You can compare the sidearm with the forehand technique in table tennis. The disc is guided at the side of the body.

### - Position
Stand with your legs slightly apart. Bend the leg on the same side as your throwing arm (like at a sidestep).

### - Grip
Put the fingertip of your ring-or middle finger into the rim of the disc. The thumb is on the upper side of the disc. The disc should be firmly in your hand. The finger in the rim of the disc gives the spin.

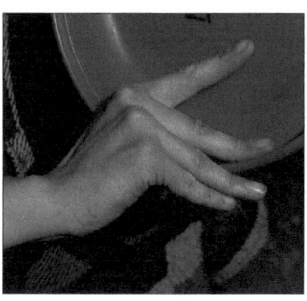

It is important that the fingertip is positioned correctly in the rim.

For this throw the disc is also held at a slanting angle.

17

### - Technique

Bend the throwing arm at
the elbow.

Take a swing with your arm from
behind. Guide the arm in a forward
direction at the side of the body,
until the arm is stretched. Give the disc
a spin with a movement from the wrist
and with the finger in the rim. Release the
disc at shoulder height in the direction in
which the disc should fly.

## 2.3 Upsidedown

Like the name says, with this throw the disc flies upside down.

### - Position
Stand easy, with the leg on the throwing arm side positioned behind (so the whole body can work like a spring).

### - Grip
The grip is the same as with the sidearm. Hold the disc at a slant here, too.

## - Technique

Take the disc firmly in your hand. Use the ball-joint of your shoulder and swing out widely (from behind taking the throwing arm over your head).With this throw the disc is released over the head. Release the disc at a slant above your head in a forward/upward direction..Using the wrist and with the finger in the rim you give it spin.

If you imagine you want to throw the disc over a 2 meter tall person, who is standing in front of you, it makes it easier at the start.

## 2.4 Roller

The roller is the basic throw to start training with the dog. Like the name says with this throw the disc rolls over the ground, so it is perfect for introducing the new toy to the dog.

### - Position
You can stand, crouch down, or kneel as you like.

### - Grip
As for a backhand

### - Technique
Roll your wrist round with the disc so that the disc is situated on your lower arm. Now give the disc spin from the wrist. Release the disc in a forward direction towards the ground. Move your arm forward so that the disc does not just crash to the ground in front of you.

The three above throws are basic throws. When you are able to throw them correctly, you can achieve different trick throws.

**All three have the following in common:**
- until they  work perfectly, you have to practice a lot... (unless you are a natural talent)
- during all three throws you can see from the way the disc flies, what you should correct in your technique
- if the disc tilts to the side it has to be held at more of an angle at the moment of release

**A disc flying like this is dangerous!**

- if the disc flies too far to the left or right, you have released it too early or too late
- Would it be possible to cut the lawn with the disc? Release the disc at a higher level.
- Does it fly too high? Release the disc at a lower level.
- Does it waver in the air? Give the disc more spin and if necessary hold the disc more firmly.
- Do you slam the disc onto the ground? Relax your grip on the the disc...

Well, now you know what you can do if you are bored. The more often you pick up the disc and play with it, the more familiar the disc will become to you.
I will later describe how to use these basic throws for trick throws. For now just practice these three throws and read how you can start to train your dog.

## 3. The dog and the new toy

**Before we start: Every dog is different!**
Even dogs from the same breed are different in the way they learn, play, move and concentrate.
This means that you should observe your dog closely from the start, to find out what it is like, what special habits it has and what abilities it already has. If you make this effort you will for the mostpart spare yourself disappointment due to wrong expectations.

### 3.1 The first step is always the hardest

Let us assume that your dog does not play with everything and everyone. This means we have to arouse its interest in the disc!
- put the food in the disc instead of in the dog bowl
- in summer you can use the disc as a bowl for water when you are out and about.
- Sit next to your dog and roll the disc away from him. Because of their natural instinct to chase their prey most dogs run after things that move away from them.
- Play with the disc on your own without involving the dog. If it shows interest offer the disc to it. It is important to pack away the disc when interest is at its highest level. Dogs are like little kids: They want what they cannot have.
- You can also play with someone else and let the dog watch you so that it can catch the disc if it wants.
- You can even become creative. Attach a cord to a disc and pull it after you so that the dog regards it as prey.
- Play tugging games

There are no limits to your fantasy. Just take care that you do not expect too much from your dog. A few minutes are enough.
And very important: acknowledge every step in the right direction, even if it is just a very small one, with loads and loads of praise!!
Your dog wants to please you and your task is to show him that he is pleasing you!

## 3.2 Start throwing

Now you have made your dog familiar with the disc. And ideally he is already enthusiastic about the disc.

Then you can start throwing (after you have practised beforehand, of course).

You start with the roller. Here the dog learns to pick up the disc from the ground while it is rolling. This way it does not have to jump after the disc straight away. And you can practice the correct retrieval if your dog does not bring back the disc. Use a long lead for this. Hold it loosely so that your dog does not suffer a jolt around the collar when it runs off, but so that you are able to bring the dog back to you gently using the lead. If your dog is good at catching rollers and in retrieving the disc, continue with short backhand throws.

Teach your dog straight away to walk around you so that it is standing in the direction of the throw. This makes things easier. Keep the throws short, so that the chance for the dog to catch the disc in the air is higher. With long throws it is often a problem that they hit the ground before the dog can catch them, so that the dog does not really have a sense of achievement. Don´t let your self get worked up by your dog! Even if it is really demanding, keep the game calm! You are the one who commands the game, not your dog! Furthermore your throws will be more successful if you throw calmly and correctly. Both of you will have more fun if the throws are successful!

Have you already mastered the sidearm?

Perfect! Then alternate between backhand and sidearm throws!

And play tugging games every now and again. You can thus encourage your dog's instinct to chase its prey and it learns that the game takes place with you. Don´t let yourself be fooled into picking up the disc yourself if the dog does not bring it back. He should bring it! If he does not … stop the game! If the dog wants to play it will quickly grasp that it has to bring the disc back.

**Don´t forget to stop the game at the right time because you are enjoying yourself so much. It is you that starts and stops the game!**

## 3.3 Playing with several discs

Now start to bring a second disc into the game. If you play too long with just one disc it is difficult to bring an additional disc into the game at a later stage.The dog is then too fixated on one disc. Therefore teach your dog a short, concise command to leave the disc. So that you can decide where and when your dog has to leave the disc. With several discs you can bring more flow into the game.

Furthermore your dog learns to concentrate on you. If the game becomes to frenzied, calm the game down..A frenzied dog is not able to concentrate.

If your dog has accepted the game with several discs,you can rotate between roller, backhand and sidearm. Have you trained the upsidedown throw too? If so, let´s go! Bring that into the game too.

So now you know the basics of discdogging. You can occupy your dog wonderfully well with these.

**Are you having fun?**

**You want more?**

**Fine!!**

Now we come to the tricks, trick throws and jumps.

# 4. Trick throws

With the basic throws backhand, sidearm and upsidedown it is possible to perform lots of trick throws. They bring variety into the game, are fun and look fantastic.

## 4.1 Backhand behind the back

- **Grip**

Like for a backhand

- **Technique**

Pass the disc around behind your back. Step forward with the opposite leg to your throwing arm (if you throw with the right hand, then with the left leg )!Release the disc. Because of the step forward you do not block yourself during the release.

Lara already knows the movement and knows what comes next.

## 4.2 The chair

### - Grip
As for a backhand

### - Technique
As if you are throwing the disc behind your back, you just close your legs, crouch down and throw around your legs.

**Bandit is standing well in the throwing direction.**

## 4.3 Backhand flamingo

### - Grip
As for a backhand

### - Technique
As with the throws above. For the flamingo you stand on one leg with the other leg stretched up/backwards or sidewards. The disc is led round the leg, on which you are standing, from behind and then released. If you throw with the right hand, stand on the right leg.

## 4.4 Sidearmflamingo

- **Grip**

As for the sidearm

- **Technique**

As for the flamingo you stand on the leg on the same side as your throwing arm. You throw this flamingo behind you from in front of you.. You should take a look behind you to see where the disc goes to.

**...for agile discdoggers...**

**3...**

**2...**

**1...mine**

## 4.5 Kick

### - Grip
For a kick hold the disc the way you do for a backhand. Then give the disc spin, so that it hovers in the air. This is the so-called floater.

### - Technique
Now you just need to hit the disc with the outer edge of your foot (kick it away) so that the disc flies! To make it even more fun, you can first throw the disc around your back or through your legs etc.

**Hitting the disc is not that easy**

## 4.6 Brushing

### - Grip
Depending on the throw.

### - Technique
The grip is not important. Brushing is plainly and simply when you push the disc away. If you throw a floater, try to shove the disc with your fingertips or your palm on the rim so that the disc flies on.

You need to have the right feeling for brushing otherwise it can be painful.

Jetman cannot wait. He is already so excited and any minute he will catch the precious flying object

**Even here it is a question of accuracy**

**Will he catch the disc?**

There are some more parts of the body where you can brush or kick the disc. For example on your knee, your chest, your lower leg.

## 4.7 Knee kick

### - Grip

Hold the disc like as for a backhand, only vertically.

### - Technique

Give the disc spin so that it does not fly away but hovers in the air in front of you. Now kick the disc with your knee. It´s just a matter of practise until you find the right point where the disc jumps off well.

**Lara flips to catch the knee kick**

# 5. Tricks

Some of the tricks are without a disc. But you can combe them very well with a subsequent throw. If you are familiar with dogdancing you will already know some of them.

## 5.1 Weave

You already know the weave poles for practising agility.We replace the poles by using our legs. Let your dog sit or stand right by your side. Take one step with the leg on the side opposite your dog. Lure your dog through your legs with the disc or a goodie.
Let the dog take its time. For many dogs it is unfamiliar to have a human standing above them.

**For every step in the right direction: PRAISE your dog!!!**

Over time you can add more and more steps so that it becomes a slalom.

If you use the disc to lure your dog you can also work with two discs. You show one, whilst holding the other behind your back so that your dog cannot see it.
In this way you can bring speed into the slalom without switching the discs from one hand to the other.

## 5.2 Roll over

**This describes the  program here.**

Let your dog lie down. Take a goodie or a toy. Hold it in front of your dog's nose but it must not be allowed to get it.

Does it want it? Good. Now pass it around behind your dog's head. This is the way you lead your dog into a roll over. When it is near to rolling onto its side, lead your dog's body on with your free hand. Most dogs do not like to lie on their back in front of the leader of the pack. If you realize that the dog stops as soon as it is almost on its back ,give it some help with slight pressure with your free hand do not use any force). Even here every step in the right direction deserves a lot of praise!
Connect the procdure straight away with a command.

Does your dog love lying on its side? You can train it to roll over from this position too. It is often easier this way.

Over time you will no longer need the goodie or toy. Then the command will be enough. Now you can also start to increase the distance. Soon your dog will roll over even if you are 5 meters away. You can also connect the command with a visible sign. For example, if you tilt your head to the right or to the left your dog will roll over without a word!

If the roll over works correctly you can go on.

Let your dog lie down. Then you should lie down opposite it. Now you can both roll over at the same time.

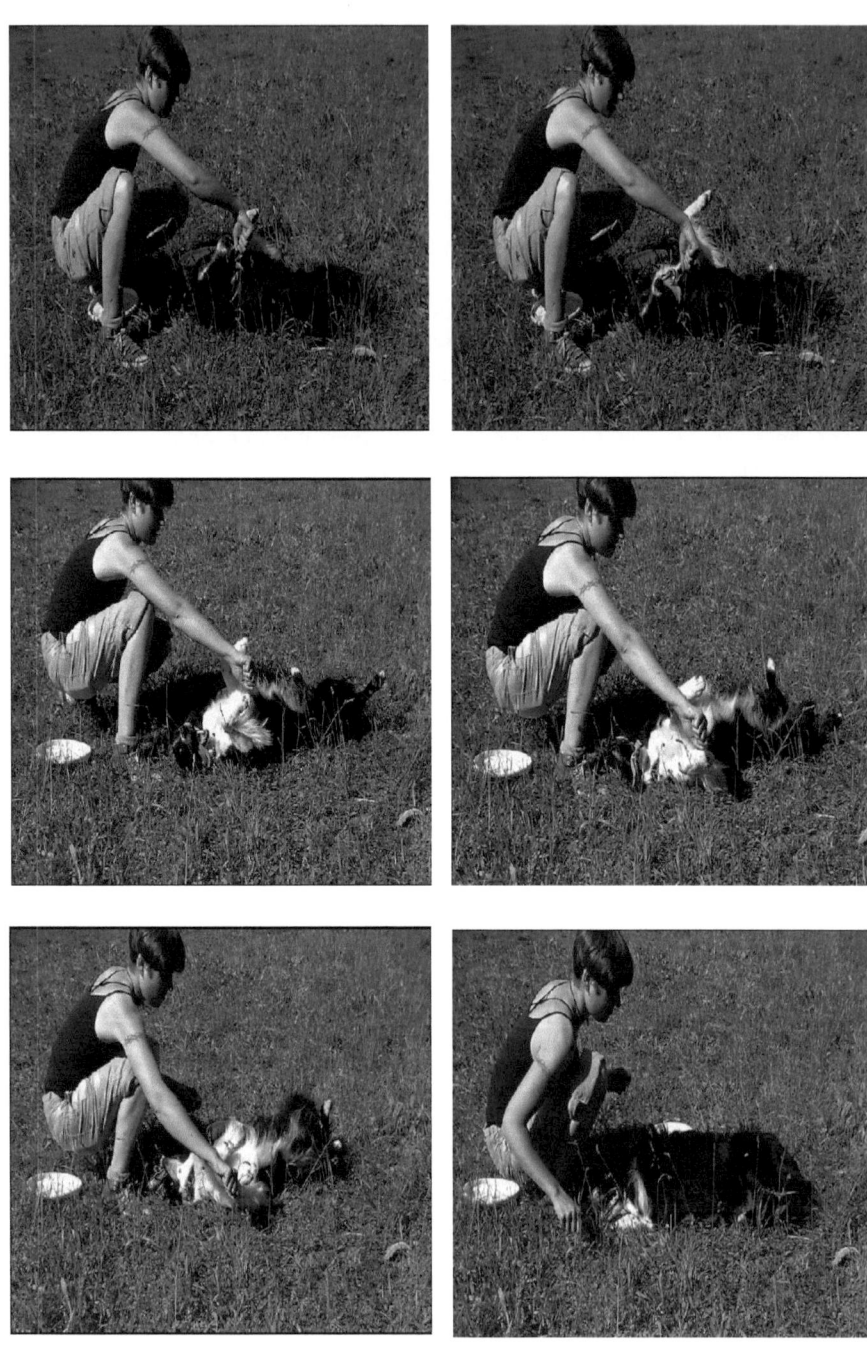

Let your dog lie down beside you. You are standing. While your dog rolls over you jump over him.

**Coordination, timing and trust.**

## 5.3 Twist

Here the dog should turn around on its own axis.

Begin to lead your dog into the twist with a goodie or a toy without it being able to get it. If it completes the twist it gets the reward and **PRAISE**.
Again connect the action with a command.
Practise the twist to the right and to the left side. Like humans dogs have a favourite side. So your dog will prefer his favourite side. With enough practise and patience it will twist in both directions.

If the twist is successful you can let your dog catch the disc coming out of the twist.

## 5.4 Hoop

For the hoop you form a ring with one arm and leg.

You need a good sense of balance!!

Hold the disc with your free hand. Your dog should be on the other side of the hoop and jump through.
At the same time it should catch the disc.

At the beginning let your dog take the disc out of your hand. Later you can throw a floater so that your dog can catch the disc while it jumps through the hoop.

If you give spin to the disc so that it hovers in the air, it is called a floater. Give a lot of spin to the disc from the wrist. The disc should hover in the air and not fly in a particular direction.

**Don´t forget to release the disc in time!**

48

## 5.5 Butterfly

Hold the disc so that the upside is showing towards your body. The disc rests on your fingers and the thumb props it up on the upside.

With the butterfly the disc rotates on its horizontal axis.

How do you achieve this?
Give the disc a forward push with your thumb pulling back your hand at the same time.

The butterfly is not a spectacular throw, but your dog has to show concentration and skill to catch the disc.

Come on! I'll catch you one way or another!!

## 5.6 Dogcatch

For the dogcatch you catch your dog in the air as he jumps. Because not every dog likes to be carried, start to get it used to this by picking him up and carrying him. Many dogs are not allowed to jump up at their owners. For the dogcatch you have to get it used to this kind of intentional body contact again.

Start by sitting down on the ground with your dog next to you. Then let it sit on your lap. Connect the action with a command right from the beginning. If this works, heighten your sitting position over time so that your dog has to jump onto your lap. If that works too, start to practise it while you are standing. Make sure that you are standing firmly, because even a small dog can really knock you over.

If your dog now jumps up at your command, you need the right timing to catch it in the air. Catch it with both arms and praise it a lot!! Of course with some dogs it is easier to use the disc to start. But bear in mind that you then have to manage both the disc and catching your dog. I personally find it is easier to practise first without the disc.

After the dogcatch make sure that your dog has a safe landing on the ground. Some wriggle so much on your arm that they nearly fall flat on their nose or injure their legs when you let them down.

A steady stance and timing are very important.

## 6. Jumps

The jumps are what make discdogging really interesting for many people. Especially if they look spectacular.
Unfortunately most of them overlook the fact that jumps are very strenuous for dogs. Try it yourself. Take off your shoes and socks. Stand on a chair and jump down.

You will then say:" That's not so bad"
Sure, a chair is not that high.
Do it again a few more times.
It does start getting unpleasant.

Of course, a dog's body is built differently. But you do not let your dog jump just one or twice. If you practise a jump, you do it several times until it works.

**What am I trying to say?:**

I do not want to talk you out of jumps. I and my dog enjoy them too. My dog is a great jumper.
I just want to open up your eyes so that you realize that behind every jump there is a lot of training, even if it looks simple.

To keep the risk of injuries as low as possible, every jump should be built up step by step. Like this you can reduce/avoid after-effects, because the necessary muscles are built up and the dog learns to jump and land correctly.

So, let's take it slowly!

**Basics:**

- Every jump, at no matter which height, should not be steep. Otherwise an unnecessary strain is put on the joints.
- The dog should not rush into the jump. It is o.k. to take a run-up, but senseless rushing makes it impossible to control the jump.
- A jump should not have a bend. The dog can easily turn in the air so that it cannot land safely.
- Teach your dog a command for starting the jump. In this way you can avoid crashing together.
- Avoid being hectic. A hectic dog does not concentrate.
- Even if your dog is a good jumper... begin with low and controlled jumps.

**In discdogging jumps are divided into vaults and overs.**

- **Over**

The dog jumps over a part of a person's body

- **Vaults**

The dog uses a part of a person's body as a launching pad.

For a vault the dog jumps higher. A safe start to the jump is very important so that the dog does not slip and have a bad landing or even fall over.

O.k. this is enough of the basics.

What's the best way to start?

## 6.1 And again not every start is easy...

Start by sitting on the ground with your legs stretched out. Let your dog sit on the right or left side of your legs.
Take the disc in the opposite hand. If your dog is too enthusiastic about getting the disc you can use something else to attract it and use the disc later.

But it is better to use the disc right from the start and to let sit the dog quietly before continuing the training. Now let your dog jump over your legs and let him take the disc out of your hand. Praise it! Repeat this till it works. When it works well raise the leg that is farthest away from the dog. This way your dog has to stretch itself during the jump and does not jump too steeply.
Now you can vary the jump height if you kneel, crouch, stand or stretch one leg for your dog to jump over.

## 6.2 ...More groundwork

And because you are on the ground anyway... start to get your dog used to standing on your stomach. With the help of another person you can get it used to standing on your back too. This is necessary if you want it to vault later.

Lie down and lure your dog with a goodie on your stomach or with the help of another person on your back. Praise your dog for each paw it sets on you.

Bear in mind that your body is an unusual area for your dog. Give it time to get familiar with it. When it has got used to it and stands on you with all four paws, practise until it becomes quite normal. Then start to place your body higher so that your dog has to jump up. It also has to get used to this. So give it time.

Now you have the basics and can continue.
Here is a small selection.

## 6.3 Over

### 6.3.1 Overleg

You have already started with this jump before. It is left to your own judgement whether you stretch your leg forwards, backwards or sideways and at what height.

First of all it is important that your dog jumps properly.

Nice jump

**Good jump off**

The hoop is an over too.

## 6.3.2 Over arm

Let your dog jump over your arm instead of over your leg. Here it is also up to you in which direction and at what height.

**Lara lifts her legs well so that she clears the jump.**

### 6.3.3 Over knee

Bend the leg which your dog has to jump over.
You can kneel or stand.

### 6.3.4 Over belly

Let your dog jump over your belly. You can lie on the ground or make a bridge.

**Nice stretching from Kirra in a flat trajectory.**

### 6.3.5 Over back

This is the jump over your back. It is best to start this over with the help of a second person.

Practise throwing the disc with this second person but without your dog ).

When you are sure your throw works, then start with your dog.
Place your dog behind you. The helper stands on the opposite side. Now take your position. Ensure that you have a firm foothold.

The helper holds the disc so that your dog can catch it easily during the jump.

Ready?

Now give the dog the jump command. After a while you can hold the disc by yourself . If this works too, then start throwing the disc so that your dog can catch it in the air.

## 6.4 Vaults

### 6.4.1 Back and front vault

Your dog has already become accustomed to body contact for vaulting. And with the over your dog is familiar with working on your body.
Now comes the stage when you teach your dog to jump off your body. For a jump off your back or belly your dog first has to learn to stand on it. The dog has to get used to feeling your body under its paws. This works best with the help of a second person.

Use goodies at the beginning. Start as low down as possible. Praise your dog at every step.

**It is always hard at first...**

**But for food it's worth a try**

When your dog can stand safely on your back and belly, increase the height so that your dog has to jump off. Here a second person is of great help,concerning your dog's safety when jumping off your back. Always let your dog stand briefly because if it jumps up to jump off, it will be difficult to achieve a safe vault.

Not until your dog can stand safely and wait for what to do next does the disc come into the game. Again it is best to have a second person to help.

Here too you should first practise throwing the disc with the other person but without your dog.

The second person holds the disc and you give the command for jumping off. Let your dog stand for a short time. The second person has to hold the disc so that the dog can catch it during the jump. And the disc has to be held at such a height and distance that the dog is encouragaed to jump off your back/ belly.
Ensure you have a good foothold for a backvault...your dog can knock you off balance really easily.
Do not practise the vault too often...remember your dog's joints,ligaments and bones. When your dog can jump off your back or belly correctly, then start throwing the disc yourself.

This needs good timing!

You have to throw the disc high enough at the right moment so that your dog is able to catch it in the air and has to jump down from you to catch the disc.

**...and ...action!**

## 6.4.2 Catapult

The catapult is also a vault. For this you stand on one leg whilst the other one is bent.

Your dog should jump from the bent leg to catch the disc. Because you have already practised overs, your dog will jump over the bent leg with no problem.

But how you get your dog to jump from this leg??
It is really quite easy.

**You need a good sense of balance for a catapult.**

You just have to hold the disc so high that your dog is not able to reach it with a normal over. Dogs are very smart, if they want something, they quickly realize that they just have to use your bended leg as a launching pad to catch the disc.

**Nice jump**

First let your dog take the disc out of your hand. When your dog can do the catapult correctly you can throw the disc with a floater.

**Here you can see how Lara is pushing herself from the upper leg.**

### 6.4.3 One more small tip

- wear thick clothes for practising vaults…unless you want to have a scratched body… even light dogs leave nice traces behind!!

- Make sure that your clothes are not slippery . Otherwise your dog cannot stand and jump off safely.

- Your clothing should not be too loose. Otherwise your dog can easily become entangled!

**Fine, now you and your dog are able to do a lot. There are many more tricks, throws and jumps. But there is just not enough space to mention them all here.**

The sport of discdogging is growing, so I´m sure you will find teams to train with. You can be creative yourself too!! There are no limits to your fantasy, as I mentioned before, except where the safety and health of your dog are concerned.

At the beginning I mentioned that you can play discdogging just for fun or with the ambition of taking part in competitions too. If you did not know before what would be right for you and your dog, perhaps you have found out while reading and practising.

If you have decided not to take part in competitions, I hope I have managed to give you some new ideas for your walks. Perhaps you are willing to compete in a team playing against other teams at championships…let´s go!

If you want to know what awaits you at a competition…take a look at the internet links below.

**But first:**

All that you have learned up to now can be combined. There are alot of possible combinations so that playing with your dog never becomes boring.

# 7. Competitions

There are different organisations holding competitions and every organisation has its own rules.
It would take too long to mention them all here. For more information you can find the internet addresses in the appendix.

All rules have one thing in common:

**The safety of the dogs is most important.**

## 7.1 Disciplines

The most popular disciplines are Minidistance (Throw and Catch) and Freestyle.
Faraway (LongDistance) is not played very often.

You can find which disciplines are offered by looking in the conditions of each competition.

Usually a competition consists of 2 rounds freestyle and 1 round minidistance.
There are also fun competitions and playdays to go to.

At competitions there is usually a minimum of three judges who judge the performance of each team. The rules state what the judges are looking for in particular.

At fun competitions and play days it is up to the host  whether the performances are judged or not.

The following rules are from the U.F.O.

## 7.2 Minidistance ( Throw and Catch )

Playground:

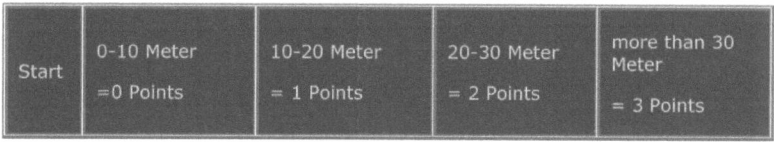

| Start | 0-10 Meter<br>=0 Points | 10-20 Meter<br>= 1 Points | 20-30 Meter<br>= 2 Points | more than 30 Meter<br>= 3 Points |

In the Throw and Catch Round competitors are given 60 seconds in which to complete as many throws as possible with one disc. At the start the dog and the thrower are situated behind the line. When the thrower indicates that he or she is ready, the line judge signals to the announcer that the competitor is ready. Then the start official counts down „3 - 2 - 1 - go" and starts the clock with the word „go". Throwers must be behind the line for all throws, but they may move around the field freely between throws. If the thrower steps on or across the throwing line at the time of the release of the disc, the throw will not be counted. If, during a round, the competitor believes the disc has become unsafe for the dog to catch because of a broken rim or a large tear, it may be handed to the judge for replacement. The damaged disc must be handed to the line judge before a replacement is given, but time will not be suspended during a disc change. A countdown of the remaining time is given at 30 seconds, 10 seconds, 5, 4, 3, 2, 1, and time. A throw is scored as long as the disc leaves the thrower's hand at the moment when or before time is called.

It is up to the team if it tries to get as many points as possible with long throws or more short throws.

## 7.3 Faraway ( Long Distance )

The team has three throws. The longest throw caught in the air is counted. Each throw is measured, i.e. the distance in meters from the startline to the point where the back legs of the dog touch the ground.

## 7.4 Freestyle

Freestyle routines have a time limit of 120 seconds and each team can perform with music to show their tricks and throws.

- different throws
- tricks with discs
- over
- vaults

Competitors may use up to 7 discs during their freestyle routine
There are no limits to your fantasy, as long as the safety and health of the dog are ensured.

Points are given for:

- **the dog owner:** different throwing techniques
  creativity

Different elements are judged, repeated actions are not

- **the dog:** athletics
  motivation
  ability to catch
  control in the air and in landing

- **the team:** Teamwork
  managing the discs
  interaction between handler and dog
  Showmanship

**Drive and Athleticism** - Judges look at the athletic ability of the canine competitor with special consideration for the dog's level of prey drive, speed, stamina, tracking skills, leaping ability, and control while in the air and during landings. Canines should show consistency while catching discs with varying spins and orientations over a range of distances.

**Ingenuity** - Judges look at the creativity, athleticism and throwing ability of the human half of the team with special consideration for the consistent placement of discs, and ability to deliver a variety of difficult throws. Successful completions are an important part of this category, but emphasis is placed on innovation and variety, not execution and repetition.

**Sequences and Flow** - Judges look at how the team works together to present a routine that flows naturally from trick to trick with smooth transitions between sequences. Individual sequences should be composed of tricks that logically flow together, and competitors should pay close attention to proper disc management when linking sequences to form a routine. Solitary tricks that are not part of an obvious sequence are given consideration for their contribution to the flow of the routine as a whole. Teams are not penalized for taking time to set up tricks properly provided the overall momentum of the routine is not compromised.

**Comprehensive** - Judges score the general impression of the routine as a whole with special consideration for showmanship, presentation, energy, and overall crowd appeal.

**Catch Ratio** - A mathematically determined number that is obtained by dividing the number of completions by the number of attempts, multiplying by 10, and then rounding to the nearest tenth of a point.

Safety: The judges can deduct up to 5 points if canine welfare is endangered.

For most discdoggers freestyle is the supreme discipline. But for the all over result of a competition it is minidistance which mostly makes a winner, because to get points at Minidistance is an art in itself. If you get a low score in Minidistance you have no chance, even if your freestyle routine has been perfect!

For Freestyle it is handy to have a routine. so that you have a better flow. Of course you can just go onto the field and just freestyle with your dog too,. for example: people like me, who always forget their routine on the field!

You will find out what suits you and your dog most.

## It is most important that you both have fun!!!

# 8.Appendix

Discdogging is becoming more and more popular all over the world. So take a look around you and I´m sure you will find some discdoggers to play with at competitions or clinics.

A variety of information can be found on the internet.

At the end I have given a list of internet addresses.

It only remains for me to wish you a lot of fun with your dog and the disc!

## Let´s rock the disc with your dog!

Yours

Julia Zimmermann

**Internet addresses:**

U.F.O.
www.ufoworldcup.org

Fundogteam Karlsruhe
www.fundogteam.de
www.fundoginfo.de

Discrockers
www.discrockers.de

USDDN
www.usddn.com

Skyhoundz
www.skyhoundz.com

Quadruped
www.thequadruped.com

FDDO
www.fddo.org

Author: Julia Zimmermann
Illustrations: H.-P. Losert
Translation help: Sally Laws-Werthwein
Thanks to Nadine Schott for supplying the pictures.